POWER-UP
TEAM GUIDE

Examples of
Process
Improvement
&
Problem
Solving

William L. Montgomery, Ph.D.

Illustrated by
Dale Schierholt II

Illustrated by Dale W. Schierholt II, Red Brick Design, Hopewell, NJ 08525

Printed in the United States
First Printing January, 1995

Published by The Montgomery Group.

ISBN   0-9641124-0-X

Library of Congress Catalog Card Number 94-96139

Acknowledgment

The idea for this Supplement to *Power-Up* started during a discussion with several creative people at GOAL/QPC in Methuen, Massachusetts. My sincere thanks to Lisa Boisvert, Robert Page, Richard Morrison, and especially to Michael Brassard for his integrating contributions to the content. Also, Tom Hartman of the Shared Services Center in Harrisburg provided valuable ideas and contributions. Finally, my thanks to Suzanne Boone for her excellent word processing and her creative ideas. Thank you all.

A Note for the Reader

This book is a supplement to two separate books:

- *Power-Up Teams and Tools*, and

- *Memory Jogger II*

Examples of teamwork and process improvement are shown here that demonstrate the methods and tools in each book above. The objective is to provide detailed insights into various approaches for *process improvement, tools, and team interactions*. Please see the Introduction of this book for more information.

Table of Contents

The Cat grinned a little wider.

"Could you tell me, please, which way I ought to walk from here?"
asked Alice.

"That depends a good deal on where you want to get to," said the
Cat.

"I don't much care where------," said Alice.

"Then it doesn't matter which way you walk," said the Cat.

Alice in Wonderland
by
Lewis Carroll

Introduction

Seven elements are important for truly effective Process Improvement and Problem Solving. Teams are effective when they have:

1. An understanding of tools.
2. An understanding of some set of Process Improvement and Problem Solving steps.
3. Data reflecting both process performance and customer requirements.
4. Teamwork, including a team leader, facilitator, and process owner.
5. Support from within the organization.
6. Ways to standardize the improvements within the process.
7. A flexible learning approach rather than a rigid one.

Of these seven, the last area - flexibility - is probably the most important because it facilitates pulling together the other six. No formulas apply to team process improvement efforts. There is no single right way. Two teams working to improve the same process will likely have somewhat different flow charts and data displays, yet both will likely make the same noticeable improvements.

This book demonstrates these seven areas through comprehensive examples of team experiences and successes. Two examples are presented, each using a different set of process improvement steps; showing that different approaches can be equally effective.

The first example demonstrates reduction of cycle time in a service organization. The team uses the Dynamic Process Improvement Method, also called the Generalized Method, which is discussed on page 14 of *Power-Up Teams and Tools* (which we will refer to simply as *Power-Up*.)

The second example demonstrates reduction of costs associated with rework and rejects in a manufacturing company. The team uses a set of steps designed around Plan, Do, Check, and Act, as described on page 115 of the *Memory Jogger II*.

These two different reference books, *Power-Up* and the *Memory Jogger II*, with their two different sets of process improvement steps, were chosen to demonstrate that teams can have flexibility in *how* they investigate a process. The common denominator for teams lies in the tools and their effective use. *Power-Up* is the companion to this *Team Guide*. *Memory Jogger II* is a pocket-sized guide to construction and use of tools published by GOAL/QPC.

Many of the data display tools covered in each book are the same. The *Memory Jogger II* has additional tools on statistical process control (SPC) such as Control Charts, and Scatter Diagrams along with all of the Seven Management and Planning tools. In addition to the data display tools, *Power-Up* has tools on team support such as the Supportive Action Matrix, and Planning Sheets, plus it has selected Management and Planning tools.

This *Team Guide* demonstrates effective use of these tools and effective team communication regardless of the particular steps used for process improvement or problem solving. *It addresses ways of thinking and proceeding, not one set of steps.* The steps used in your organization may be very similar to any of the steps found here, or may have only some similarity. As long as the steps used in your organization are effective, we encourage you to use them and make them a standard in your company. This book is written for any organization, any set of process improvement steps, and any process improvement team.

The table below summarizes the examples provided in this book:

Name of Company	Type of Company	The Problem Area	Process Improvement Method Used	Reference for the Process Improvement Method
Steve's Country Store	Service	Cycle Time	Generalized Method	*Power-Up*
Global Container Productions	Manufacturing	Rework	PDCA based	*Memory Jogger II*

Both companies used in the examples are fictitious. The processes and the improvement activities, however, are similar to many situations we find in service organizations and manufacturing companies.

Let's get started!

Service Example

The following example is representative of processes that arise in service companies and in the service or administration sections of manufacturing companies. Service companies can include health care, insurance, banking, transportation, repair, education, and more. General service processes that occur in many types of organizations and companies include marketing, sales, order placement, contracting, scheduling, shipping, and even research and development.

Service involves contact with a customer. Often, as in the example here, there is only one employee making that contact. The speed, accuracy, and overall successful service provided by that employee depends on support from other functions that the customer may not see, but the employee must have. *Processes are a chain of functions that lead to a contact and an outcome for the customer.* Each part of the chain is important, but the end person in the organization does not always have control over the whole. Let's begin the example.

STEVE'S COUNTRY STORE, A STUDY IN CYCLE TIME

Shoppers at Steve's Country Store were waiting in long lines to pay for their merchandise. The store had over ten thousand items, including groceries, gifts, household appliances, farm supplies, and more. The functions of the cashier seemed simple enough, yet the lines were long and people were complaining. The store had five lines. Steve tried adding more checkout lines, but that simply led to additional long lines. Competition in the next town seemed to do better with checkout time and Steve was concerned. At the same time, he has always wanted the store to be seen as a friendly, low technology country store with old-fashioned appeal. He does not want scanners.

A team was formed with two cashiers, along with one of the store managers and the head cashier, Kathy. Bob, who had read *Power-Up Teams and Tools*, the *Memory Jogger II*, and some other books on quality tools, was asked to be the facilitator. He asked Steve to provide books for all team members, which Steve did. The team chose to use the Generalized Process Improvement Method described on *Page 14* of *Power-Up Teams and Tools*.

My Ideas and Items to practice at the next team meeting

....

A table summarizing the Generalized Method for process improvement, and the tools that can support each of the stages, is shown below:

Six Stage Generalized Process Improvement Method

For more information on this six stage method, see Page 14 of Power-Up.

STAGE OF PROCESS IMPROVEMENT	PRIMARY ACTIVITIES	SUGGESTED TOOLS
STAGE 1: SCOPE	o Decide on the process to address o Determine the boundaries o Determine team members o Determine process owner	o Brainstorming o Affinity diagram o Customer-Process-Supplier Model o Basic data displays, such as Pareto Chart, Bar Chart, etc. o Planning Sheet
STAGE 2: FLOW	o Describe the flow of the process o Identify inefficiencies and bottlenecks o Begin identification of key data collection points	o Column Flow Chart (also called Deployment Flow Chart) o Basic Flow Chart o Analysis Tools for Flow Charts o Data display tools
STAGE 3: CUSTOMER / SUPPLIER	o Determine customer requirements o Determine the requirements of the process on the inputs from suppliers	o Interviews o Requirements matrix o Data display tools
STAGE 4: ISSUES	o Collect, display, and analyze data o List problems or opportunities o Select one issue to address at this time	o Various data display charts: pie, bar, run, Pareto, radar, histogram o Flow charts o Decision matrix
STAGE 5: CAUSE	o Identify possible causes o Verify with data o Identify root cause	o Cause-and-Effect diagram o Data display charts
STAGE 6: SOLUTION	o Generate possible solutions o Run a trial, if necessary o Implement o Standardize	o Brainstorming o Affinity diagram o Decision matrix

My Ideas and Items to practice at the next team meeting

....

....

MANAGING THE MEETINGS

Kathy, with Bob's help, used the *P.A.R.T.* - Purpose, Roles, Agenda, Time - to plan the meetings. The P.A.R.T. template is provided in the Appendix of *Power-Up*. For the first meeting she sent a notice to team members and to supporting managers. The notice had the following P.A.R.T. attached:

P.A.R.T. for First Team Meeting

Purpose:
1. To review the six stages of the general process improvement method, also called the Dynamic Process Improvement Method:

Scope, Flow, Customer/Supplier, Issues, Cause, Solution

2. To establish the boundaries of the checkout process.
3. To complete a Planning Sheet that captures our goals and any needs we have as a team.

Agenda:
Clarification of store goals - Steve.
(Steve will be at this meeting the first half hour)
Review of the general process improvement approach.
Construct Customer-Process-Supplier Model
Review of any customer complaints we have.
Complete Planning Sheet.

Roles:
Team Leader - Kathy
Scribe for first meeting - Ron, Cashier
Facilitator - Bob

Time:
August 1; 12 noon to 1:30 in the small lunch room.

For more information on this P.A.R.T. see the Appendix of Power-Up.

My Ideas and Items to practice at the next team meeting

....

....

STAGE 1

SCOPE

STAGE 1: SCOPE

At the first meeting, the team constructed the *Customer-Process-Supplier Model* discussed on Pages 46 and 47 of *Power-Up*:

CPS MODEL

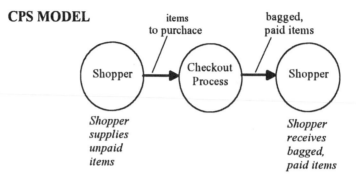

Boundaries

The above model allowed the team to see and agree on the boundaries of the checkout process. Until this drawing, discussions were:

> "Should we include the people that stock the shelves as being inside the checkout process? They put labels on items and could be considered part of the checkout process."

> "How about the people that update the review sheets for special items? We us those sheets in our checkout process and if they are wrong, it can delay our work. Aren't those people part of the checkout process?

These were great questions. *The checkout process could indeed be defined as starting at some earlier point than this team decided.* They chose, however, to limit the scope in order to investigate their part of the checkout steps. They reasoned this way: "If the problem turns out to be primarily with the lack, or inaccuracy, of input information that cashiers receive from other functions in the organization, that will become clear during the study and the problem can be addressed."

Customer as the Supplier

Notice also that the team discovered a case where the supplier and the customer are the same - in this case it is the store shopper. Perhaps 20 percent or so of all service processes are such that the supplier and the customer are the same. It is not unusual. The implication of such a situation in a corporate setting is that if a customer says, for

My Ideas and Items to practice at the next team meeting

....

....

example, "I want this information package on time and completely accurate", then the process owner would be saying to the supplier (perhaps the same person) "I need this raw data to be on time and accurate!" The customer's desire for quality output may depend on their supplying quality input.

Process Owner

Based on this model and their decisions on the boundaries, the team selected the process owner as the head cashier, Kathy. In turn, Kathy needed to talk to Steve about the extent of the authority she would have in this effort. Yes, this was a discussion about *empowerment*. Kathy told Steve what she needed to do the job, as far as she could tell right now, and Steve gave her some groundrules on the time frame for completion, and on the amount of money the team could spend in a solution. He said he wanted to avoid "those lasers that read bars".

For more information on the Process Owner, see Pages 5 and 44 of Power-Up.

Data

The team created a Pareto Chart (Chapter 10) based on the customer complaints to the service desk over the previous two months. That chart is shown below.

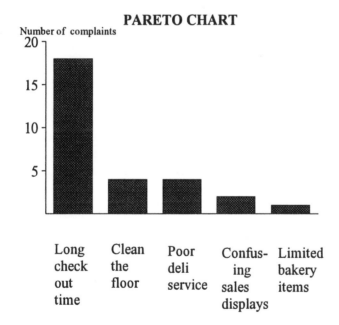

PARETO CHART

Pareto Chart
Page 143 of Power-Up

Page 95 of Memory Jogger II

This data confirmed for the team that the main problem area was the amount of time the shoppers wait in line. *The team also realized that they had no data on the specific requirements of shoppers.* They only had the complaints shown above.

My Ideas and Items to practice at the next team meeting

....

....

STAGE 1

SCOPE

Planning Sheet

See Appendix

of Power-Up

Planning Sheet
The team established their goals and documented their plans by using the Planning Sheet in the Appendix of *Power-Up.* They wrote the following statements on their Planning Sheet:

PLANNING SHEET ITEMS

Goals of Team :
- To make a reduction in checkout time within eight weeks that is so noticeable that it causes the complaints to be cut in half.

- To then reduce the checkout time even further as part of continuous improvement. Targets to be determined later.

Needs of Team:
- To gather data on the checkout times and on customer requirements.

- To continue discussions with Steve about his expectations and the decision level of the team and of Kathy. This will be an ongoing communication about empowerment of the team as issues arise.

Outcomes and Learning Points of the Scope Stage
The team constructed a Pareto Chart confirming the checkout process as the one to improve, established the boundaries of the checkout process, and identified a process owner. They clarified their team goals, and the immediate needs of the team. They practiced a structured way of running their meetings with a P.A.R.T. and with a Planning Sheet. They also began a discussion with Steve on the empowerment of Kathy and of the team.

Tools Used

- P.A.R.T.   • Customer-Process-Supplier

- Pareto Chart   • Planning Sheet

My Ideas and Items to practice at the next team meeting

....

....

STAGE 2: FLOW

The team agreed that they needed a flow chart for several reasons:

- They needed to make the steps in the checkout process visible for themselves. Their discussions and decisions would only be as good, Bob the facilitator pointed out, as the information and common understanding that they have.

- Flow charts would help the team plan the collection of data, which they very much needed.

- Flow charts would allow them to share their plans and findings with others in the store.

- Flow charts would allow the team to document the improvements they recommend for the process.

Column Flow Chart (also called Deployment Flow Chart)

Kathy and Bob had previously trained the members in constructing the flow charts. They wrote a P.A.R.T. for the meeting on flow charting. All team members were asked by Bob to read-up on flow charts before the meeting. The P.A.R.T. stated the purpose of this meeting as shown below:

Purpose: To construct a flow chart of the checkout process.

To begin analyzing that flow for delays that may lead to long time periods for shoppers.

To plan collection of data.

The team wanted to understand the flow at a macro, or high, level before getting involved in details. They decided to begin with a Column Flow Chart (Chapter 2 of *Power-Up*). *They began with the input and output items shown on their CPS Model from the Scope Stage.* Also, they recognized that two *basic* inputs, review sheets and labels, were needed by the checkout process. (Basic inputs -page 47 of *Power-Up* - are needed by the process but are not changed by it. Real-time inputs are changed. The items for purchase were real-time inputs.) Review sheets were used for special items of the week. The team constructed the following macro flow in about 30 minutes:

My Ideas and Items to practice at the next team meeting

....

....

STAGE 2

FLOW

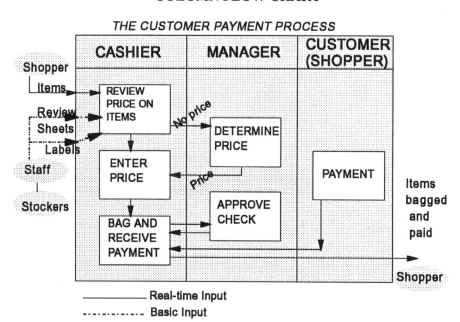

COLUMN FLOW CHART

THE CUSTOMER PAYMENT PROCESS

The team then decided to analyze the Column Flow Chart by using a Table of Internal/External Customer Requirements, which is discussed in Chapter 4, Tools for Analyzing Flow Charts, of *Power-Up.* Ron agreed to gather data and construct the table. He presented the table on the next page to the team which they accepted into the meeting minutes.

My Ideas and Items to practice at the next team meeting

....

....

TABLE OF INTERNAL/EXTERNAL CUSTOMER REQUIREMENTS

Subprocess Output	Customer	Customer Requirement	Customer Target	Perceived Actuals	Perceived Gap
Price request	Manager on duty	Clarity of the request	100%	100%	Little or none
(Same)	(Same)	Few requests each day	2 or 3 each hour	5 to 15 each hour	Large ☑
Price from manager on special items	Cashier	Speed	One minute or less	One to two minutes, usually, but sometimes much longer.	Uncertain (Need more data)
Request for check approval	Manager on duty	Few requests each day	2 or 3 each hour	5 to 8 each hour	Medium ☑
Check approval	Cashier	Speed	One minute or less	One to two minutes, usually.	Uncertain (Need more data)
Bagging	Shopper	Speed and Care	Two minutes or less	Much longer when talking or out of bags	Occasionally slow

For more information on this tool, see Page 69 of Power-Up

From the above table the team began to suspect the 'Determine Price' subprocess and the 'Approve Check' subprocess of being 'time eaters'. In both cases the volume of requests exceeded the internal customer's target (the target of the manager on duty), and could be responsible for delays, but they realized that they needed more data to verify their suspicion.

The team agreed to:
> *(1) First talk to shoppers about specific requirements. This meant they would move on to Stage 3 at this time.*
> *(2) Later, in Stage 4, collect data on process performance:*
> > ○ *Overall checkout time*
> > ○ *Time to determine price*
> > ○ *Time to approve checks*

My Ideas and Items to practice at the next team meeting

STAGE 2

FLOW

Meeting Notes and Evaluations

The team decided, with Bob's encouragement, to use the Meeting Notes template in the Appendix of *Power-Up Teams and Tools*. The Meeting Notes were placed on the bulletin board in the lunch room. Further, the Meeting Evaluation sheet also in the Appendix was used to capture improvement opportunities in the running of meetings. Both Kathy and Bob were open to the feedback. The team decided to use the evaluation sheets at the end of each meeting and to use a Bar Chart (Chapter 8) to track the results.

Outcome and Learning Points of the Flow Stage

The team established the Column Flow Chart of the checkout process. Using a table to analyze the flow chart, they began to see that two particular subprocesses of that overall flow could be 'time eaters'. They agreed to construct a more detailed flow chart at a later time when that detail might be useful. All of their decisions and key points were captured in Meeting Notes, and meetings were evaluated to facilitate improvements in running those meetings.

Tools Used

· P.A.R.T.   · Column Flow Chart

· Table of Internal/External Customer Requirements

· Meeting Notes Template   · Meeting Evaluation Sheet

My Ideas and Items to practice at the next team meeting

....

....

STAGE 3: CUSTOMER / SUPPLIER - Requirements
The objectives of the team in this stage were to learn about:
- Requirements from customers
- Requirements (of the checkout process) on suppliers

They began with the customers.

Requirements from Customers
The team needed more information from the shoppers in the store, and they recognized the need to have the information in a measurable, quantifiable way. They needed requirements for maximum waiting time, and on other service issues that the customer cares about.

Bob, the facilitator, pointed out the Customer Requirements Matrix in Chapter 5 of *Power-Up*. The team decided that it was the right tool to capture their customers' requirements because it shows:
- What the customer wants, and a description of it.
- A measurable target the customer has.
- The relative importance of each item to the customer.

Interviews
The team realized that interviewing shoppers was the only way they could capture reliable information for the Customer Requirements Matrix. They also realized that interviewing itself can be a project, so they adopted the Plan - Do - Check - Act (PDCA) approach (see the Preface of *Power-Up*) to conducting the interviews.

P: Planning the Interviews (as part of PDCA)
As they planned the interviews with the customers, the team addressed several important issues. In particular, they planned what they would say at the **beginning** of the interview:
- The length of the interview - 1 minute.
- The purpose - To improve checkout service.
- The appreciation of Steve's Country Store for the shopper taking the time.

The team then planned and constructed a few interview questions using the *Customer Requirements Matrix* as a guide for writing the questions:
- What services are important to you during checkout?
- How can you tell that you are receiving each of those services?
  (How would they measure it?)
- What would be good performance? (What 'target' do they have?)

My Ideas and Items to practice at the next team meeting

....

STAGE 3
CUSTOMER,
SUPPLIER

• How important is each service?
• How are we doing? (Gap)

D: Doing the Interviews (as part of PDCA)

The interviews were conducted as shoppers left the store. The team interviewed 50 shoppers, 20 on a weekend, and 30 during the week.

As a small 'thank you' they offered the shoppers a pin-on button like the one shown here.

Based on the interviews, the team was able to construct the *Customer Requirements Matrix* shown below:

Customer Requirements Matrix

Page 81 of Power-Up

CUSTOMER REQUIREMENTS MATRIX

The Checkout Process

Output from Checkout Process	Quality Character-istics	Descrip-tion	What to Measure	Target	Import-ance to Customer	Customer view of gap	Rank
Service	Timely	Time for checkout	Minutes to checkout	Less than seven	4	4	16
	Courteous	Personal treatment during checkout	# of complaints	None (zero)	3	1	3
	Accuracy	Charge	# of errors	None	5	1	5
		Change	# of errors	None	5	1	5

Ratings: 1 = low, 5 = high
(For example, a '1' on gap means a small gap, or deviation,
from what the customer expects.)

My Ideas and Items to practice at the next team meeting

....

....

D: Doing the Interviews (continued)
During the interviews, shoppers made comments typical of these few:
> "This is a friendly store with good products. I don't mind being in a line with five people in front of me as *long as it moves*."
> (The shopper's emphasis in italics)

> "I like the small store feeling here, but that is changing as the store grows. I am most annoyed by waiting for price checks. In the early days, cashiers knew the price of everything. Now I stand waiting while someone tries to find a price."

> "I like labels, I like seeing the price. But sometimes I get hung up while checking out."

During construction of the Customer Requirements Matrix, the team experienced and discussed the following points:
- Time required for checking out was brought up by 38 people. That was more than any other Quality Characteristic.
- The required, or expected, time for checkout varied among shoppers, but it was never more than 10 minutes. Some said , "Ten minutes once I'm at the register is too long!"
- Most of the desired checkout times given by shoppers was 5 to 8 minutes.
- The average of all the requested times was about 7 minutes.
- The overall ranking of 'Timely' was significantly higher than for other shopper requirements, which meant that the length of time for checking out was important to shoppers *and* they perceived that it was not being handled well (a fairly large gap).

C&A: Check and Act on the Interviews (as part of PDCA)
The team evaluated the effectiveness of the interviewing project by asking:
- Do we have sufficient data?
- Do we have the right data?
- Can we draw a conclusion from this data?
- Were shoppers interested and cooperative in this approach?

They decided that the answer to each question was "yes!"   Seeing no need to redo or modify the interviews, they decided there was no need to 'Act' (to Modify or Change), and moved on to drawing conclusions from the Customer Requirements Matrix. Those conclusions are listed on the next page.

My Ideas and Items to practice at the next team meeting

....

STAGE 3
CUSTOMER,
SUPPLIER

Conclusions from Customer Requirements Matrix
Earlier, in Stages 1 and 2, the team had little data on shopper expectations. Now they had solid information. The team wrote these conclusions in their meeting minutes:

- Shoppers enjoy the friendly nature of our store.
- In the Checkout Process there are three areas shoppers especially
  care about -
  - Timely checkout once they have reached the cash register.
  - Courteous service during checkout.
  - Accuracy of being charged and in the change they receive.
- The only area of current concern is timeliness of the checkout.
- Most shoppers want to be in and out of the cash register area in 7 minutes or less.

The team shared these results with all the cashiers, the managers and Steve. Everyone was interested in the results. Some cashiers said, "I try to get people through as fast as I can, what can I do?" Steve assured them that this study was not about individuals, it was about the process. Something was wrong with the system of checking out shoppers. Bob reminded people of the Column Flow Chart and said, "The problem is somewhere on this flow chart. We have *time eaters* in this process that slow down the cycle time, that is, the checkout time. We need to find those time eaters and find out why they are happening so we can fix them!"

Requirements on Suppliers
A team member asked Kathy, the team leader: "*When do we make our requirements on our suppliers clear?*" Together they looked at the Column Flow Chart to remind themselves who the suppliers were for this Checkout Process. Note, the idea was not to list suppliers to the whole store, like wholesalers and others, but only the suppliers to the process under study. Those suppliers were (see the Column Flow Chart on page 10):

- Shoppers - they supply the items into the checkout process
- Staff - they supply review sheets used to look up some items
- Stockers - they supply the labels on the items

When the team next met at lunch time, the questions Kathy asked were, "Are we receiving what we need from each of our suppliers? Are our requirements for input to the checkout process being met?" The team chose to use a Table of Internal/External Customer Requirements which is discussed in Chapter 4 of *Power-Up*, and was used by them earlier in Stage 2. They compiled this table in about 15 minutes:

My Ideas and Items to practice at the next team meeting

....

....

TABLE OF INTERNAL/EXTERNAL CUSTOMER REQUIREMENTS

Process Input	Customer (Internal)	Customer Requirement	Customer Target	Perceived Actuals	Perceived Gap
Review Sheets with prices for selected items. Supplier is Staff.	Cashier	Up-to-date prices	100%	Very high.	Little or none
(Same)	Cashier	Complete. No item missing that is supposed to be on the sheets.	100%	Very high.	Little or none
Labels on each item. Suppliers are the Stockers.	Cashier	Most items have labels. Around 90%	100%	Most items have labels.	Uncertain

STAGE 3
CUSTOMER,
SUPPLIER

For more information on this tool, see Page 69 of Power-Up

In answer to Kathy's questions, they wrote:
- Shoppers - yes
- Staff   - yes
- Stockers - uncertain

The term 'uncertain' meant that the team did not know if their input requirements were being met.

The team now had two areas to understand better through data collection:
- 'Time eaters' inside of the checkout process - from Stage 2
- The quality of the inputs to the checkout process - from this Stage 3

They began to see these two areas as being closely related. Namely, if the inputs were a problem, that could be causing extra time inside the process. The long cycle times that occur could be due to poor quality of the inputs.

They decided to move on to Stage 4, Issues, in order to explore both time eaters and input quality.

My Ideas and Items to practice at the next team meeting

....

STAGE 3

CUSTOMER,

SUPPLIER

Outcomes and Learning Points of the Customer/Supplier Stage

The team conducted a successful interview of 50 shoppers and constructed a Customer Requirements Matrix.   From the matrix they concluded that one area within the checkout process was of concern to customers, and that was timeliness of passing through the cash register area. Customers wanted a 7 minute or less checkout interval. On the supplier side, they concluded that they needed more information to determine if their requirements of suppliers were being met.

Tools Used

- Interviewing, with a PDCA approach   • Customer Requirements Matrix

    • Table of Internal/External Customer Requirements

- The following tools were used at all meetings and can be found in the
  Appendix of *Power-Up Teams and Tools*:
    ○ P.A.R.T.
    ○ Meeting Notes
    ○ Supportive Action Matrix (Chapter 15 and the Appendix)
    ○ Evaluation Sheet

My Ideas and Items to practice at the next team meeting

....

....

STAGE 4: ISSUES

The objective of the team at this stage was to identify one issue or problem in the process to fix. This one issue had to have significant impact on the checkout time.

Data Collection

From their work in the previous Stages, the team had two action items for this stage of their investigation:

   A. Data was needed on the time required for a shopper to checkout.
   B. Data was needed on each of the suspected 'time eater' subprocesses.

They began with action item 'A'.

Checkout Time

The team decided to collect separate data for weekends and weekdays. They selected Friday, Saturday, Sunday, and Monday; four days total. Five shoppers would be selected at random during two-hour intervals between 8:00 am and 6:00 pm each day. The store hours are 8:00 am to 10:00 pm, but they felt that little more would be gained by collecting data after 6:00 pm.

Supportive Action Matrix

The manager on the team, Loret, volunteered to collect the data on action item 'A' above, but the other team members expressed concern that their fellow cashiers would think that she was measuring them instead of the health of the process itself. Instead, Judy, one of the cashiers on the team, volunteered. The Meeting Notes stated:

> The cashiers may believe that they are personally being watched, when in fact the objective is to measure and understand the overall process. To explain the purpose of the measuring, all of the team members will be involved in talking one-on-one with the other cashiers. Judy will actually collect the data, but if a cashier not on the team expresses an interest, they will be invited to participate. Data collection will take place over four days starting this Friday.

The Supportive Action Matrix (Chapter 15) was used to capture the above agreements. Judy was directly supported, or helped, by Loret, and that was also captured on the matrix, as shown on the next page:

My Ideas and Items to practice at the next team meeting

....

STAGE 4

ISSUES

Supportive Action Matrix

Page 211 of Power-Up

SUPPORTIVE ACTION MATRIX (SAM)

Task	Assigned to	Support from	Date Assigned	Planned Completion Date	Measure of Success	Review Date	Comments
Collect data on time in line	Judy	Loret Help with ideas and collection	August 16	August 22	At least 100 shoppers, randomly selected. Time measured for each shopper.	None needed	Inform cashiers first. Study period will be August 19 through August 22

This matrix made the task and measure of success clear for everyone.

Based on the SAM above, Judy and Loret collected data on 25 shoppers each of the four days, as shown below and on the next page:

Weekend Customer Checkout Time (in minutes)

Customer #	8-10 am	10-12 am	12-2 pm	2-4 pm	4-6 pm
(Saturday) 1	2.5	3	6	5.5	4.5
(Saturday) 2	3	4.5	12	7.5	2.5
(Saturday) 3	1	5.5	11	7.5	11
(Saturday) 4	5	5.5	11.5	9	9
(Saturday) 5	4.5	12	8.5	6.5	8.5
(Sunday) 1	4	8.5	9	15	4.5
(Sunday) 2	3.5	6.5	6	6	6.5
(Sunday) 3	1	13	5.5	7	4.5
(Sunday) 4	2	1.5	4.5	8	5.5
(Sunday) 5	2	1.5	10	14.5	12
Average	2.9	6.2	8.4	8.7	6.9

My Ideas and Items to practice at the next team meeting

....

....

Weekday Customer Checkout Time (in minutes)

Customer #	8-10 am	10-12 am	12-2 pm	2-4 pm	4-6 pm
(Friday) 1	7	2	7.5	7	6
(Friday) 2	3.5	8	8	9.5	4.5
(Friday) 3	4.5	5	8.5	3.5	5
(Friday) 4	2	4	5	2.5	3.5
(Friday) 5	5.5	4.5	4.5	6.5	5.5
(Monday) 1	6	7	6	5	6.5
(Monday) 2	7.5	9.5	6.5	2	5
(Monday) 3	6.5	8.5	7	4.5	7
(Monday) 4	4.5	8	5.5	7.5	5
(Monday) 5	5	6.5	9	8.5	8
Average	5.2	6.3	6.8	5.7	5.6

The team then used each data point from the two tables above to construct Run Charts (Chapter 9 of *Power-Up*). The average time for completed service was 6.6 and 5.9 minutes, respectively, as shown on the following two Run Charts:

RUN CHART

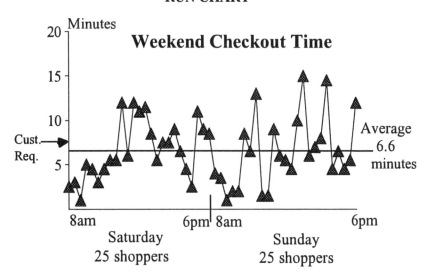

Run Chart
Page 127 of
Power-Up

Page 141 of
Memory Jogger II

My Ideas and Items to practice at the next team meeting

RUN CHART

STAGE 4

ISSUES

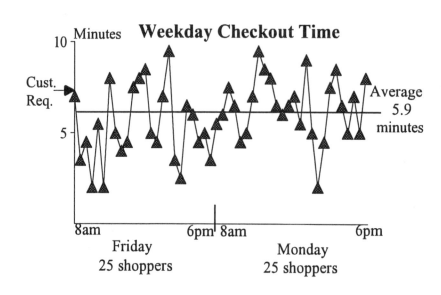

A team member said:

"The customer requirement is 7 minutes. We average about 6 minutes! We are doing better than the requirement!

Another said:

"Watch out for the average! Remember Chapter 15 of *Power-Up*. Every data point above 7 minutes on the Run Chart represents a potentially unhappy customer! If we plot a Histogram, I think we will see the problem more clearly."

The team plotted an overall Histograms following the ideas in Chapter 11 of *Power-Up*. They simply counted the number of shoppers by one minute time intervals and plotted the values in vertical bars. The resultant Histogram is shown on the next page:

My Ideas and Items to practice at the next team meeting

....

....

HISTOGRAM

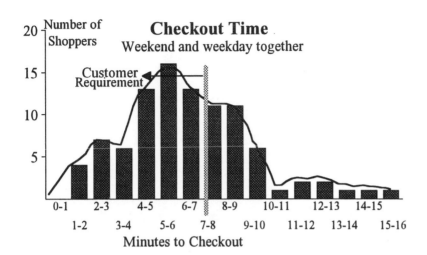

"Wow!", said one team member. "Almost half of the 100 shoppers are over the 7 minute mark!"

The team displayed the same Histogram this way:

HISTOGRAM

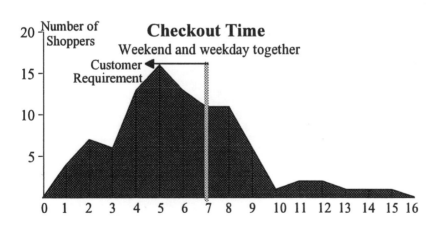

My Ideas and Items to practice at the next team meeting

STAGE 4

ISSUES

To determine how much of a difference there might be between weekends and weekdays, they constructed separate Histograms:

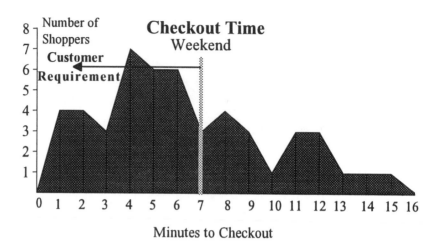

Histogram
Page 157 of
Power-Up

Page 66 of
Memory Jogger II

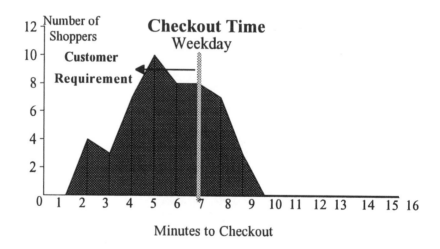

My Ideas and Items to practice at the next team meeting

....

....

From these Histograms, the team concluded:

- *"Both weekends and weekdays show the problem, but weekends show significantly longer times."*
- *"Our initial objective of cutting complaints in half could probably be achieved by cutting 3-4 minutes off of the longer checkout times".*

Kathy drew the sketch below and said to the whole group, "If we can achieve a Histogram like this over the next few weeks, customers will certainly notice the difference."

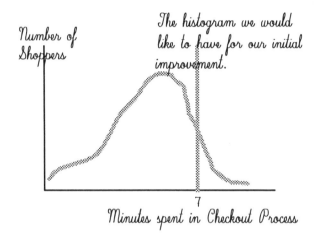

Number of Shoppers

The histogram we would like to have for our initial improvement.

7

Minutes spent in Checkout Process

Time Eaters

To achieve a shorter cycle time, or checkout time, the team turned its attention on the second objective stated at the beginning of this Stage 4; the 'time-eaters.' They knew from analysis of the flow chart in Stage 2 that checking on prices was the largest time eater, and check approval was another. They began with price checks by collecting data on:

- Number of price checks each hour
- Time required to complete a price check

Only weekends were studied because weekends showed the worst checkout times. The Bar Chart and the Run Chart on the next page display the data uncovered by the team.

My Ideas and Items to practice at the next team meeting

....

....

STAGE 4

ISSUES

BAR CHART

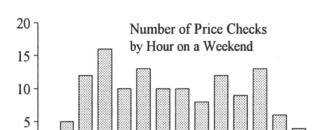

The chart on the left shows the number of price checks requested of the manager on duty on a weekend. Both Saturday and Sunday were included in the study, then the number for each hour was averaged for simplicity. The values for each day were close, so the team was comfortable averaging the two.

RUN CHART

The chart on the right shows the minutes spent on each price check for the first ten in each hour. Only three hours are shown for simplicity. The team had other data, but this chart is representative of what they found during busy hours and non-busy hours.

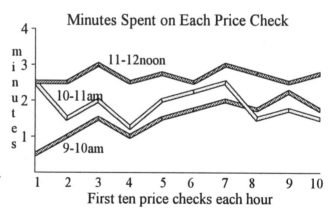

Similar charts were made for the check approval function, but the frequency of requests and the durations were about one-third of those for price checks.

The team now knew for certain that a significant 'time eater' was the price checking function in the process.

My Ideas and Items to practice at the next team meeting

....

....

PARETO CHART

The team then needed to know why price checks were initiated. Why did cashiers have to call on managers for prices on items? What were the main reasons? That inquiry led to this Pareto Chart on the right.

This Pareto Chart allowed the team to see the one issue to address in the next stage. Their objective had been to find one primary issue, and they had.

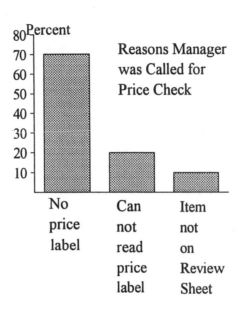

The Issue Statement in the Meeting Notes read:

> "Price labels are missing from items, causing overload on managers and delays in checking out."

One team member reminded the group that the priced labels are not simply white glue-on labels. The labels are special order items that were selected to give identity to the store. The labels looked like this:

Steve's Country Store

Price _____

My Ideas and Items to practice at the next team meeting

....

STAGE 4

ISSUES

Outcomes and Learning Points of the Issues Stage

The team established with a Histogram that the customer requirement of 7 minutes or less was not being met for a significant proportion of shoppers, especially on the weekends. The Histogram clearly showed the spread beyond 7 minutes, even though the average checkout time was less than 7 minutes. The team saw how misleading an average can be. Through further data collection and the use of a run chart and bar chart, the team also established that the price checking function of the manager on duty was a primary 'time eater' in the process. Further, the primary issue, and the one selected to address was 'Price Labels Missing from Items'. That issue, made clear with a Pareto Chart, caused the need for many price checks and resultant delays.

Tools Used

· Supportive Action Matrix (SAM)

· Histogram   · Bar Chart   · Run Chart   · Pareto Chart

My Ideas and Items to practice at the next team meeting

....

....

STAGE 5: CAUSE

The team's efforts were now beginning to focus faster. The objective at this stage was to find the primary, or root, cause of labels missing on items.

Kathy issued a P.A.R.T. (Appendix of *Power-Up*) that had this statement as the Purpose for the next meeting:

> Purpose: Find the root cause of the absence of price labels from store items reaching the checkout line.
>
> We expect to use the Cause-and-Effect Diagram. Please review Chapter 13 of *Power-Up* before the meeting.

Two people that stock the shelves were invited to this meeting because they have experience with the whole system of ordering the special labels and placing them on items with prices entered on those labels.

Review to Date

The purpose of this next meeting, with the team members and the stockers, was to find the root cause of missing labels on items. Before that effort began, the whole group, with stockers, spent one half hour reviewing the events that brought them to this important point. They briefly reviewed:

- Customer-Process-Supplier Model
- Pareto Chart of complaints
- Column Flow Chart
- Analysis of the Flow Chart
- Customer Requirements Matrix
- Run Charts and Histograms of checkout time intervals
- Bar Charts and Run Charts on the Price Checking function
- Pareto Chart showing the 'missing labels' as most frequent reason for checking prices.

After that review, they were all prepared to create the Cause-and-Effect Diagram.

My Ideas and Items to practice at the next team meeting

....

STAGE 5

CAUSE

Cause-and-Effect Diagram

At the meeting, all the team members and the two stockers gathered around the flip chart to construct this diagram:

CAUSE-AND-EFFECT DIAGRAM

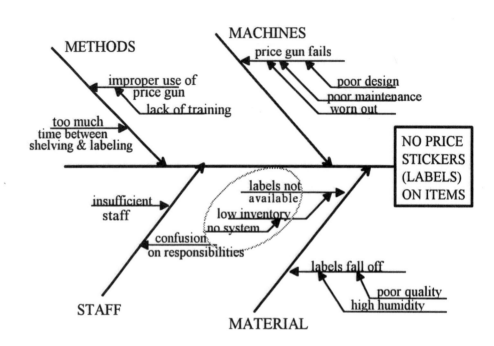

They began by placing the Issue from Stage 4 in the box on the right. The headings for the four main branches (or main bones of the 'Fishbone' Diagram, as it is often called) were the general headings that are often used. Those worked well for them, the team concluded. They constructed the possibilities based on their actual experience. This was not "blue sky brainstorming", said one person. "These things actually happen."

After constructing the diagram, Bob the facilitator asked, "What are the primary causes of all the ones we have created? Can you circle one or two?" The team all focused on one area and circled it, as shown above. The next step was to collect data to verify that the circled area was indeed the primary one.

My Ideas and Items to practice at the next team meeting

....

....

Data Verification

The team had little trouble gathering the data shown on the Pie Chart below. They simply talked to stockers, inspected items that were on the shelves, and talked to a few shoppers. Area 'A' was so large that the message was clear.

PIE CHART

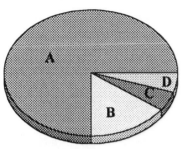

A - No labels in   75%
    the inventory

B - Labels fall off   15%

C - Price gun   5%
    problems

D - Shoppers buy
    before price   5%
    placed on item

DATA VERIFICATION OF
ROOT CAUSE ON THE
CAUSE-AND-EFFECT
DIAGRAM

Pie Chart

Page 99 of
Power-Up

The team had found a primary cause of delays and customer complaints. They wrote this statement in their Meeting Notes:

Primary Cause

Our special order pricing labels are often in short supply which causes stockers to place items on shelves without labels. The delays created by the absence of price labels is not acceptable to many of our shoppers.

My Ideas and Items to practice at the next team meeting

....

STAGE 5
CAUSE

Outcomes and Learning Points of the Cause Stage

Using a Cause-and-Effect Diagram, the team established and grouped a number of likely causes of the missing labels. During that construction effort, they learned the value of involving people who are experts in the particular issue being addressed. The stockers had firsthand knowledge of the missing label issue.

The team collected data to verify that one particular cause was the root, or primary, cause of the missing labels on items. Lack of a process to assure labels in the inventory was the primary cause of long checkout times.

Also, the team saw the interdependence between the performance of a function and the quality of the output of that function. The checkout process was slow because one of the basic inputs to it, the labels, was lacking.

Tools Used

- Cause-and-Effect Diagram   • Interviewing

• Pie Chart

My Ideas and Items to practice at the next team meeting

....

....

STAGE 6: SOLUTION
The objective of this stage appeared to be simple.

> ***The team wanted to find an effective, practical, long term, and reasonably low cost solution to solve the inventory problem with the labels.***

Each team member soon realized, however, that while the idea was simple enough, they had several criteria to meet and they were not sure how to proceed. Bob, the facilitator, discussed ideas with several people. He, too, was looking for an effective way to find a suitable solution. After several discussions, and after reading about several tools, he chose two tools that he believed would assist the team. The two tools were:

· Affinity Diagram   and   · Decision Matrix

Affinity Diagram
Bob chose the Affinity Diagram (Chapter 1 of *Power-Up*) because he wanted a tool that would automatically categorize ideas for ways to solve the inventory problem. Bob discussed the specific inventory problem with the team to be certain everyone understood the problem the same way. While an Affinity Diagram is often used to identify detailed actions that are then grouped together and categorized, the team decided that they were looking for more general and broad solutions at the moment. The details of implementation could come later. So Bob asked the team members to be fairly broad in their suggested solutions and to be creative in their thinking.

He then wrote a question based on that discussion and the team formed the Affinity Diagram on the next page. The headers at the top of each column were created last. They captured the theme of the suggestions in each column. The column on the right side was beyond what Steve, the store owner, had originally set as policy. Still, the team wanted to at least explore the value of using high technology in their 'country' store.

My Ideas and Items to practice at the next team meeting

STAGE 6
SOLUTION

AFFINITY DIAGRAM

WHAT CAN WE DO TO SOLVE OUR INVENTORY PROBLEM
WITH PRICE LABELS?

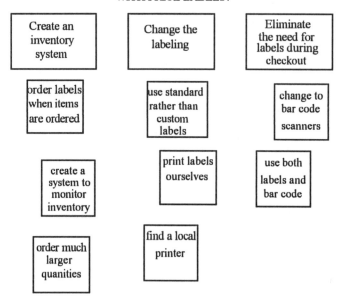

This Affinity Diagram was exactly what the team needed at this point. It provided a set of realistic choices and grouped them together for easy comparison and discussion.

Decision Matrix

From each of the columns, one solution was taken that the team as a whole agreed was representative of the others in the column. Those three potential solutions were written on the left side of a Decision Matrix (Chapter 14 of *Power-Up*), which is shown on the next page.

Next, the team discussed and summarized their criteria for use in the Decision Matrix. They accomplished this by making a list of criteria, then condensing it by combining similar items, until they had a reasonable number of criteria to address. In this case, they had four criteria, as shown on the next page. The team applied weighting to the criteria, as discussed in *Power-Up*, and spend some time obtaining cost estimates. The estimates of time saved by each potential solution came from the data collection and analysis conducted during earlier stages, especially Stage 4. After the data was collected, they used a scale of 1 to 5 to rank each potential solution for each criteria. A rank of 1 is undesirable, and 5 is desirable, as discussed in *Power-Up*.

My Ideas and Items to practice at the next team meeting

....

....

DECISION MATRIX

	Initial cost	Cost to Operate	Impact on Customer	Impact on Store Identity with Customer	Total Score
Weighting	5	5	10	9	
Order labels with items	$ 0 5 25	$ 0 5 25	save 2-3 min. 4 40	No change 5 45	135
Use standard labels	$ 0 5 25	$ 0 5 25	save 2-3 min. 4 40	Lower 2 18	108
Use bar code scanner	$50,000 1 5	$ 0 5 25	save 5 min. est. 5 50	Lower 2 18	98

Decision Matrix
Page 197 of
Power-Up

Page 105 of
Memory Jogger II

To their surprise, the team found that the bar code scanner solution had the lowest score. Ordering labels with the weekly ordering of items for the store had the highest score. Bob reminded the team of the discussion on use of a Decision Matrix in *Power-Up*, Chapter 14. Namely, if someone on the team disagrees with the highest ranking option being the one to undertake first, it may well be because they have some insight or information that the rest of the team does not know. The team discussed the scores and the criteria used and decided that they could and would support the results of the Decision Matrix they had constructed. The solution that was best for their situation was "order labels with items."

My Ideas and Items to practice at the next team meeting

....

....

STAGE 6

SOLUTION

Standardize the Solution

Ordering the special labels seemed simple enough, but there had been confusion on when to order and how many. One of the team members drew this suggested flow chart for the ordering of labels. This was the solution the team implemented.

Basic Flow Chart
Page 55 of
Power-Up

Page 56 of
Memory Jogger II

BASIC FLOW CHART

New System for Ordering Price Labels

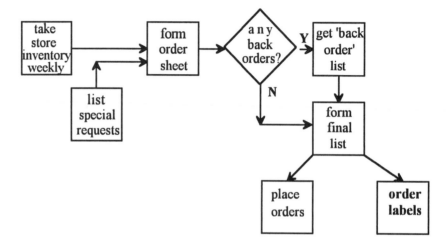

Store inventory has always been taken weekly. That part of the solution was not new. What was new in the above flow was:

- Clarity of the job of ordering store items. It had never been drawn as a flow of steps before. Now anyone, even a new employee could better understand the steps.

- Clarity on when and how to order the special pricing labels. The number to be ordered would be determined from the number of items on the final list.

My Ideas and Items to practice at the next team meeting

....

....

Implementation

The Basic Flow Chart was shared with the order department, the stockers, all the managers, Steve, and all of the cashiers. The solution was accepted and welcomed by everyone. They knew from the data that a major 'time eater' would be eliminated. Implementation was simply a matter of asking the order department to follow the flow. The stockers, in turn, were asked to contact the order department whenever labels were getting low, because that was an early warning that the new system was having a problem.

Results

The team process from the Scope stage, through generating a solution in the Solution stage took five weeks with the team meeting roughly twice a week for an hour or two. Charts were often sketched outside of meetings then brought in for discussion. That helped to save time.

The implementation of the new order system first occurred during the sixth week. After the eighth week, managers on duty and cashiers began to notice a difference in the number of price checks needed. After the twelfth week the decrease was quite noticeable.

As a follow-up Judy collected data on the number of price checks to compare to previous findings. The decrease was dramatic:

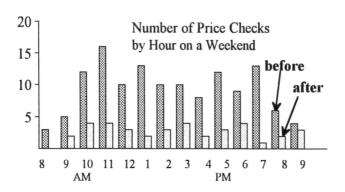

Bar Chart

Page 113 of Power-Up

STAGE 6

SOLUTION

My Ideas and Items to practice at the next team meeting

....

STAGE 6

SOLUTION

Likewise, the team compared customer checkout time before and after the change to the inventory system for labels. The results were significantly better:

HISTOGRAM SHAPES

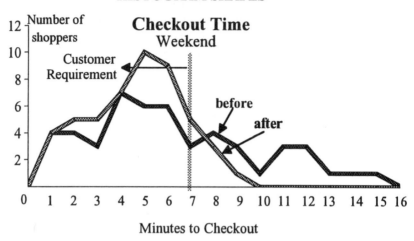

Further, customer complaints about checkout time decreased to virtually nothing. Instead, shoppers noticed the difference in not standing at the cashiers counter waiting for price checks and they expressed some delight at the faster service.

Celebration and Recognition

Steve sent a notice to all employees, both full-time and part-time, inviting them to a late night celebration after the store closed on a Saturday night. Spouses and friends were invited as well. Steve gave a short talk on the success of the team and pointed out the "new approach to managing our problems that the Checkout Team practiced and demonstrated for us." He gave each team member and the stockers that participated with the team a watch with a note that said:

> *Thanks for a fine job in reducing our checkout time.*
> *We have begun a new approach to managing our work.*
>   *Steve*

My Ideas and Items to practice at the next team meeting

....

....

Outcomes and Learning Points of the Solution Stage

The team identified and implemented a solution that was effective in reducing the checkout time. Further, that solution was the best of three in satisfying a set of criteria involving cost, customer impact, and identity of the store. They used an Affinity Diagram to explore solutions. That diagram led to use of a Decision Matrix that not only allowed the team to make a common decision, but showed them that the high technology solution would not satisfy their criteria well. Use of a Basic Flow Chart facilitated the creation and clarification of a solution to the problem of missing price labels. Finally, they implemented the solution and were able to compare performance of the checkout process before the change with the performance after by use of bar charts and histograms.

STAGE 6

SOLUTION

Tools Used

- Affinity Diagram   • Decision Matrix   • Basic Flow Chart

- Bar Chart   • Run Chart   • Histogram

Postscript

Everyone in the store saw the value of the team's work and the process improvement approach they used. As a result, the natural next step was to continue improvements using data, customer focus, and process improvement tools. Employees throughout the store began to understand that even as individuals not on a team, they could manage their jobs with this new approach.

A new team was formed to give others a chance to participate. That team addressed a system for accelerating check approval.

The motto at Steve's Store soon became:

"We are a country store improving our country ways."

End of Service Example

My Ideas and Items to practice at the next team meeting

....

"That's it, Father! interrupted Pinocchio. "We'll build a great big fire!"

"Not the chairs! warned Geppetto. "What will we sit on?"

"We won't need chairs," shouted Pinocchio. "Father, don't you understand? We'll build a big fire and make Monstro sneeze! When he sneezes, out we go! Hurry ---- more wood!"

Pinocchio
by
Collodi
and
Walt Disney

Manufacturing Example

The following example is representative of situations that arise in a manufacturing business. Manufacturing involves creating a product that must meet customer specifications. When one component or characteristic of that product is not satisfactory, the cost of rework and of handling recalls can be significant. Further, customers may not return, which means lost revenues. Isolating the section of a process flow that has difficulties is key to improving a manufacturing process. Without such process improvement, products can continue to fail inspections and customer acceptance tests, which leads to increased cost and lost revenue. This example shows how a team isolated and corrected a problem that was causing significant customer complaints and rework costs.

GLOBAL CONTAINER PRODUCTIONS, A STUDY IN REJECT RATES

The demand for cubic steel containers from GCP has always been strong. These cubic containers come in three different sizes, C-100, C-200, and C-300, where the number refers to the side dimension in inches. The containers are typically used for storage or shipping and have a hinged top. The company fabricates the containers from steel sheets that are cut, bent, attached on the edges with fasteners, and painted. There are several inspection steps. The containers are not sold as air tight, so welding is not used, which keeps the price down and allows the containers with their edge fasteners to be disassembled for shipping. The edge fasteners were designed and developed by the company founder. The fasteners are fabricated and drilled in the GCP factory.

Four months ago customers had been returning the cubic steel containers at a rather high rate. The reasons for the returns varied. Betty, in the Quality Control Group, suggested to Karl, the owner and founder of GCP, that she and a few others work together to find and eliminate the production problem. The "Boxing Team", as they named themselves, was formed with Betty, Sam who heads the assembly unit, Karen from purchasing, and Ned from the folding unit. These four were selected because they had attended a two-day workshop on Process Improvement Tools and they had expressed an interest to Karl in helping streamline the operations.

My Ideas and Items to practice at the next team meeting

....

....

The group asked if Nancy from accounting could be the team facilitator and thereby help keep their meetings and communications on track. Nancy had also attended the two-day workshop and had been trained as a facilitator at another company two years earlier. She wanted to help and was supported by her supervisor. The team had four members plus Nancy. Betty was elected team leader by the group.

THE PROCESS IMPROVEMENT / PROBLEM SOLVING STEPS

The team chose to use a set of activities designed around 'Plan, Do, Check, Act' as described on page 115 of the Memory Jogger II. That set of steps is summarized below, along with typical tools used at each step:

PDCA Activities
from
Page 115 of
Memory Jogger II

	Activities	Typical Tools
Plan	Select a Problem or a Process.	Brainstorming, Affinity Diagram, Data Displays (such as Pareto Chart, Histogram, Run Chart), Prioritization Matrix.
	Describe the Process Flow.	Deployment Flow Chart, Basic Flow Chart, Tree Diagram.
	Describe Various Causes and Identify the Root Cause.	Affinity Diagram, Cause-and-Effect Diagram, Interrelationship Digraph, Data Displays
	Develop a Solution.	Flow Charts, Activity Network Diagram, Prioritization Matrix, Matrix Diagram, Tree Diagram.
Do	Implement the Solution.	Flow Charts, Activity Network Diagram, Data Displays.
Check	Evaluate the Solution	Check Sheets, Data Displays, Flow Charts.
Act	Reflect and Act on Learnings.	Affinity Diagram, Radar Chart, Brainstorming, Affinity Diagram.

My Ideas and Items to practice at the next team meeting

....

....

PLAN: SELECT A PROBLEM OR A PROCESS

Betty sent a note to each of the team members before the first meeting. That note stated the objective for the team:

> **Objective:**   To reduce customer returns of our cubic containers.

Attached to the note was a P.A.R.T. (Purpose, Agenda, Roles, and Time) that she found in the Appendix of *Power-Up Teams and Tools* and decided to use as a guide for the first meeting:

<u>P.A.R.T. for First Meeting of the Boxing Team</u>

> **Purpose:**   Identify the problem to address.
>
> **Agenda:**   Review reasons for returns.
>   Review rates of returns.
>   Decide on a specific problem to address.
>   (We may need more data and therefore may not
>   be able to make a decision until a later meeting.)
>
> **Roles:**   Team Leader - Betty
>   Facilitator - Nancy
>   Other Members - Sam, Karen, and Ned
>
> **Time:**   First Meeting July 15, 8:00 to 10:00 am in conference room.

PLAN :
SELECT PROBLEM
OR PROCESS

First Meeting

At the first meeting Betty quickly reviewed the objective. The team then began to discuss various pieces of data that they had brought to the meeting. Karen had gathered data on customer complaints from the Customer Service Department. The team decided to review that data in an attempt to focus on a particular issue.

The Pareto Chart on the next page reflects one month of customer complaint data:

My Ideas and Items to practice at the next team meeting

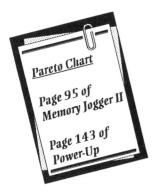

PLAN :
SELECT PROBLEM
OR PROCESS

Pareto Chart

Page 95 of
Memory Jogger II

Page 143 of
Power-Up

PARETO CHART

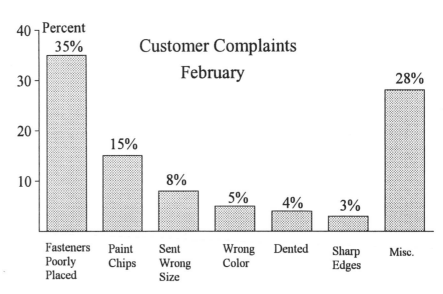

The team saw from the above chart that most cubic containers were being returned because of problems with fasteners. Sam, who heads the fasteners assembly unit said: "I'm not surprised. We have a fair amount of rework cost associated with fixing those units that are returned to us either by the inspection group or by the customer."

Nancy, the facilitator, pointed out: "That's important to know, Sam, because we may be able to save that cost with the process improvement work we do here."

Rework Costs
Betty wanted to see more data on rework costs because it could help them understand the importance of reducing rejects and could provide insights for further improvements later, as part of an ongoing effort. The team agreed that they would ask each work unit to estimate the dollars spent on reworking cubic containers during the last month. They gave themselves three days to gather the data and pointed out to the work units that they only needed estimates, not detailed accounting. At the next meeting they constructed the following Pareto Chart based on the rework cost estimates:

My Ideas and Items to practice at the next team meeting

....

....

PARETO CHART

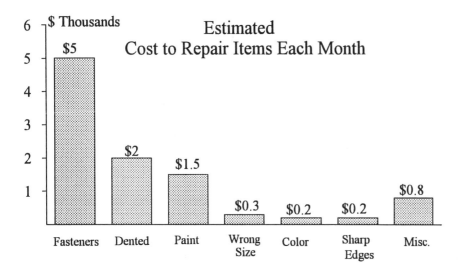

Estimated Cost to Repair Items Each Month

Type of Complaint

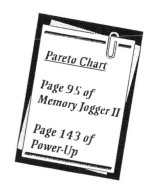

The Pareto Chart above showed the team, and the whole company, that roughly $10,000 was being spent each month on rework of rejected cubic containers. Of that amount, about $5,000 was spent fixing or replacing the fasteners on the edges.

Nancy, the facilitator, asked the group: "What criteria will we use in selecting a problem to address? Certainly the fastener problem affects our customers and our costs, but are there other considerations? Let's be sure before we automatically select the fastener problem."

The team created the following statement on a flip chart in about ten minutes:

"We will select the problem to address based on:
1. Impact in reducing customer complaints
2. Impact in reducing our rework cost.
3. Impact on improving our productivity.
4. Ease of correcting the problem, that is, can we handle it."

My Ideas and Items to practice at the next team meeting

....

....

PLAN :
SELECT PROBLEM
OR PROCESS

Nancy said that the fastener problem certainly satisfied all the criteria, but if they wanted to make their decision visible in a graphical way, a Matrix Diagram (also called a Relationship Matrix) would help. The team said that it would be useful to see the criteria compared to the problems, so they turned to page 85 in the *Memory Jogger II* and constructed the matrix below. They chose the highest four customer complaints for the left side of the matrix and compared those to their criteria for problem selection.

MATRIX DIAGRAM

	Customer Satisf.	Cost Savings	Product-ivity	Ease of Fixing	
Fasteners	◎	◎	△	△	20
Paint Chips	○	○	△	○	10
Wrong Size	○	△	△	○	8
Wrong Color	△	△	△	○	6

◎   Strong Relationship   (9)

○   Medium Relationship (3)

△   Weak Relationship   (1)

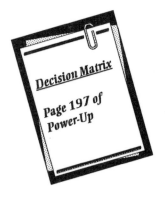

In this case, a Decision Matrix from page 197 of *Power-Up* could have been used as well. The matrix made their decision clear not only for themselves, but for others as well. They decided to address the fastener problem, which meant they would be identifying what was going wrong and how they could correct the situation.

They needed data on the degree of the problem with fasteners, and collected the following data from the inspection groups:

My Ideas and Items to practice at the next team meeting

....

....

RUN CHART

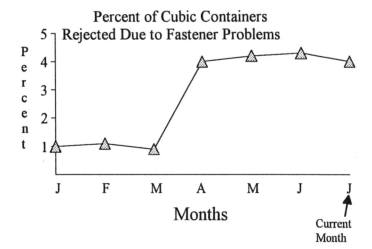

Percent of Cubic Containers Rejected Due to Fastener Problems

Months

Current Month

Run Chart

Page 141 of Memory Jogger II

Page 127 of Power-Up

Planning Sheet

Nancy suggested that the team use the Planning Sheet in the Appendix of *Power-Up Teams and Tools* as a way of documenting their objectives and plans.

Based on all of the data collected and plotted on display charts, the team wrote the following in their Planning Sheet:

Goal of the Team

Customer complaints and inspection rejects on our edge fasteners have risen sharply in the last three months. Those complaints are the highest frequency of all customer concerns and the cost to rectify the problem is our highest.

Our goal is to find the cause and to improve the process in order to significantly reduce the reject rates associated with fasteners.

Needs of the Team

To have support from the rest of the company as we gather data and construct flow charts associated with the fasteners.

My Ideas and Items to practice at the next team meeting

PLAN :
SELECT PROBLEM
OR PROCESS

Outcomes and Learning Points of 'Select a Problem or Process'
The team constructed two Pareto Charts, one of frequency by type of customer complaint, and one of cost by type of complaint. They experienced firsthand how to use the data to make comparisons of relative importance.

They clarified and documented their criteria for selecting a problem to address, and they constructed a Matrix Diagram to display the relationships between the criteria and the customer complaints. That matrix provided a graphical display of their decision process. Fasteners were found to be the largest and most significant problem area in terms of customer impact and potential cost savings to the company.

The team then constructed a Run Chart showing the percent of rejected cubic containers since the beginning of the year. A marked increase was recorded in the four months just preceding the first meeting of the team. Based on the data, the team was able to use a Planning Sheet to record their objectives and their needs.

Tools Used

- P.A.R.T.
- Pareto Diagram
- Matrix Diagram
- Run Chart
- Planning Sheet

My Ideas and Items to practice at the next team meeting

....

....

PLAN: DESCRIBE THE PROCESS FLOW

Sam, the team member from the assembly unit, had volunteered to construct a Column Flow Chart, or Deployment Flow Chart, which he found on Page 61 of the *Memory Jogger II*. Betty issued a P.A.R.T. that stated the purpose of the next meeting:

> Purpose: To review and discuss the flow chart of the process that Sam has constructed, and to analyze that flow for places where the problem could be occurring.

Sam brought the following drawing to the next team meeting:

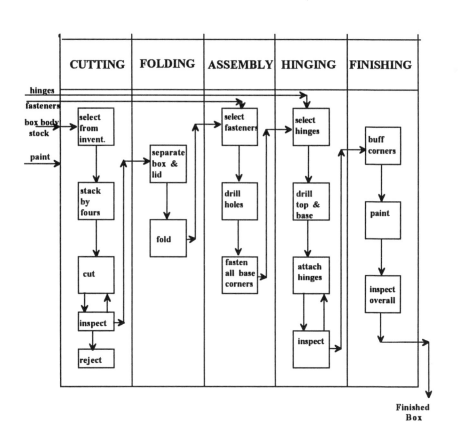

COLUMN FLOW CHART
CONTAINER MANUFACTURING

Deployment Flow Chart
Page 56 of Memory Jogger II

Page 39 of Power-Up

My Ideas and Items to practice at the next team meeting

....

....

PLAN :
DESCRIBE THE
PROCESS FLOW

The team reviewed and discussed this macro (high level) flow chart on the preceding page and agreed that it represented the steps in constructing the cubic steel containers. They agreed to make the drawing part of their Meeting Notes, and they posted the drawing on the bulletin board with a note asking for corrections or comments. All of this took less than thirty minutes.

Analysis of the Flow Chart
The team, at the same meeting, turned their attention to analyzing the flow chart. They constructed a simple Matrix Diagram which displayed the fact that fastener problems could be caused by difficulties in several functions:

MATRIX DIAGRAM

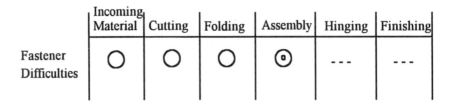

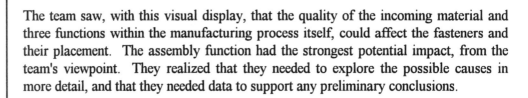

	Incoming Material	Cutting	Folding	Assembly	Hinging	Finishing
Fastener Difficulties	O	O	O	⊙	- - -	- - -

Matrix Diagram

Page 85 of Memory Jogger II

The team saw, with this visual display, that the quality of the incoming material and three functions within the manufacturing process itself, could affect the fasteners and their placement. The assembly function had the strongest potential impact, from the team's viewpoint. They realized that they needed to explore the possible causes in more detail, and that they needed data to support any preliminary conclusions.

Nancy, the facilitator, asked the team to look at the functions that could affect the fasteners again. Then she commented:

> "We have Karen from purchasing who can represent changes to be made in incoming material, and we have Ned from the folding unit, and Sam from the assembly unit. We do not have, however, anyone from the cutting unit. Should we?"

My Ideas and Items to practice at the next team meeting

....

....

The whole team discussed that issue for a few minutes. If the problem was in the cutting function, they would need a representative on their team. Ned said, however, that he knew that area well. He suggested that the team wait to understand the likely causes a bit better before adding another team member. They all agreed.

They decided to move on to the next step of solving the problem.

PLAN :
DESCRIBE THE
PROCESS FLOW

Outcome and Learning Points of 'Describe the Process Flow'
The team had never before constructed an overall flow of the process for manufacturing the cubic steel containers. They were able to see from that Column Flow Chart (or Deployment Flow Chart) the steps in the process, the interconnection of those steps, and the work units involved.

They were able to quickly see, in analyzing the flow, the possibilities for a process error or shortcoming in one work unit affecting the placement of fasteners during the assembly function. A few degrees off during cutting of an edge, for example, could cause the fasteners to fit poorly.

They also saw from the flow chart that one of the functional units that could be affecting the fastener problem was not represented on the team. They decided to gather more information before increasing the team membership. They then decided to move on to explore causes in more detail.

Tools Used

· P.A.R.T.   · Column Flow Chart   · Matrix Diagram
(Deployment Flow Chart)

My Ideas and Items to practice at the next team meeting

....

....

PLAN :
DESCRIBE VARIOUS
CAUSES AND IDENTIFY
ROOT CAUSE

PLAN: DESCRIBE VARIOUS CAUSES AND IDENTIFY ROOT CAUSE

The P.A.R.T. for the next meeting stated the purpose as:

> Purpose: To begin discussion of possible causes.
> To identify data to collect that will assist in identifying the
> root cause.

Betty's point in stating the purpose above was that the team would begin the exploration of causes at the next meeting, but they could not expect to settle on a root cause until they had collected more data. No one wanted to base a future change, or solution, in the manufacturing process on a guess of a root cause. It had to be a root cause that was verified with data.

Data on Reasons for Failures

In advance of the meeting, Betty had asked Sam if he could gather some data on the various reasons the fasteners fail inspection, and how often those reasons occur. Sam brought the data, and the team gathered around a flip chart as Nancy made this Pie Chart based on Sam's data:

PIE CHART

Reasons for fasteners
failing inspection

angle 60%

other 8%

width 12%

length 20%

Data collected by
Sam, May-July

My Ideas and Items to practice at the next team meeting

....

....

Ned asked, "Couldn't we also plot that same data on a Pareto Chart?" "Right," said Nancy, "and here is a Pareto Chart of that data." She sketched the following chart:

PLAN :
DESCRIBE VARIOUS
CAUSES AND IDENTIFY
ROOT CAUSE

PARETO CHART

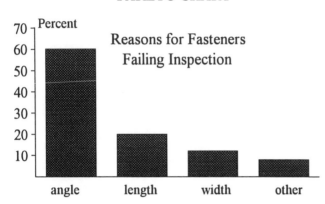

Pareto Chart

Page 95 of
Memory Jogger II

Page 143 of
Power-Up

"Well," said Ned, "I certainly see the primary cause of the fastener problem. The angle of the fasteners on the edges is out of specification range."

"Right," said Karen, "but I wonder how far off it is. Are we dealing with major misalignments, or are they only slightly out of alignment?"

"Why do you want to know the amount of deviation?" asked Betty.

"Because," said Sam, "the cause of the problem might be very different for a consistently small deviation than for a large one." They all agreed.

More Detailed Data

Karen volunteered to gather data from the inspectors on the degree of deviation. It meant a special study for about a week, but it would not be difficult. Ned offered to help and together the team filled out a Supportive Action Matrix because they felt this was data not previously gathered and studied and they all wanted to be as clear as possible. This is the matrix they entered into the Meeting Notes:

My Ideas and Items to practice at the next team meeting

....

PLAN :
DESCRIBE VARIOUS
CAUSES AND IDENTIFY
ROOT CAUSE

SUPPORTIVE ACTION MATRIX

Task	Assigned to	Support from	Date Assigned	Planned Completion Date	Measure of Success	Review Date	Comments
Collect data on angle deviations	Karen	Ned	July 25	Sept. 1	At least 50 fastener angles	Next meeting, Sept. 1	Use past records from QA group. Select data randomly.

Karen and Ned made arrangements with the inspection groups to have them record fastener angles for one week. They would measure and record the angles on 72 fasteners each day for 5 days, giving a total of 360 data points. Karen then made a column listing half degree (0.5) intervals on paper and counted the number of measurements falling in each interval. This required about 20 minutes and resulted in the following:

Degrees from vertical		Frequency
(-5.0) - (-4.5)		
(-4.5) - (-4.0)		
(-4.0) - (-3.5)		
(-3.5) - (-3.0)		
(-3.0) - (-2.5)		
(-2.5) - (-2.0)	I	1
(-2.0) - (-1.5)	I	1
(-1.5) - (-1.0)	III	3
(-1.0) - (-.5)	IIIII IIIII ------ II	57
(-.5) - 0	IIIII IIIII ---- III	98
0 - .5	IIIII IIIII ------ IIIII	105
.5 - 1.0	IIIII IIIII ------ IIIII	75
1.0 - 1.5	IIIII III	8
1.5 - 2.0	III	3
2.0 - 2.5		
2.5 - 3.0	II	2
3.0 - 3.5	II	2
3.5 - 4.0	II	2
4.0 - 4.5	II	2
4.5 - 5.0	I	1

My Ideas and Items to practice at the next team meeting

....

....

With this table on the previous page showing the frequency of deviations by measurement interval, Karen and Ned easily drew the following Histogram:

PLAN :
DESCRIBE VARIOUS
CAUSES AND IDENTIFY
ROOT CAUSE

HISTOGRAM

FASTENER ANGLE

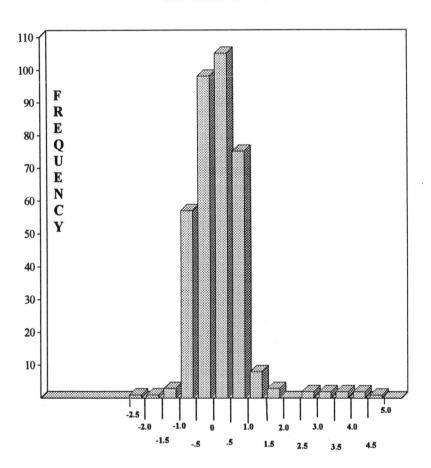

DEGREES OF DEVIATION FROM VERTICAL

The engineering specification on the angle requires the deviation to be within 1.5 degrees of vertical. Fourteen fasteners exceeded 1.5 degrees, which was about 4 percent of the 360 fasteners that were studied.

My Ideas and Items to practice at the next team meeting

....

PLAN :
DESCRIBE VARIOUS
CAUSES AND IDENTIFY
ROOT CAUSE

Next Team Meeting
Karen asked Betty to send a notice to the team asking them to be prepared for the next team meeting where they would review the data and use it to identify possible causes of the problem. The P.A.R.T. stated the purpose for the next meeting as:

Purpose: To discuss the results of Karen and Ned's data collection.
To identify possible causes with a Fishbone Diagram.
To identify data needed to pinpoint the root cause.

At the next meeting the team discussed the Histogram and the fourteen fasteners that fell outside of specification limits. They agreed among themselves that the customers were seeing this same problem and that was the primary cause for the returns and the complaints. All the data pointed to that conclusion. Their objective, they agreed, was to understand the primary reason, or root cause, of the angle deviations.

Fishbone Diagram
A Fishbone, or Cause-and -Effect, Diagram was constructed by the whole team at this meeting. They had many ideas on realistic, possible causes of the angle problem, and they were anxious to organize those ideas on paper.

They chose to use the four functional areas previously identified in the 'Describe the Process' step as possible places in the overall manufacturing process where the problem could be occurring. The Matrix Diagram from that analysis step is repeated below:

MATRIX DIAGRAM

	Incoming Material	Cutting	Folding	Assembly	Hinging	Finishing
Fastener Difficulties	O	O	O	⊙	- - -	- - -

The first four areas on the above Matrix Diagram became the categories on the Fishbone, or Cause-and-Effect, Diagram. The next page shows the diagram they created in about 25 minutes:

My Ideas and Items to practice at the next team meeting

....

....

PLAN :
DESCRIBE VARIOUS
CAUSES AND IDENTIFY
ROOT CAUSE

CAUSE-AND-EFFECT DIAGRAM

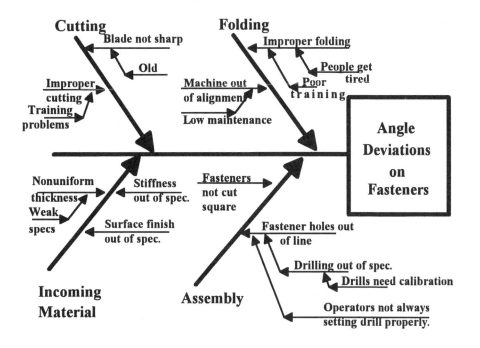

Based on their experience, the team selected three possible causes to explore further. The three areas from the diagram above were:

"Drilling out of spec." - Which meant the drilling of holes in the fasteners was sometimes outside of specification limits for vertical alignment.

"Fasteners not cut square" - Which meant that the fasteners were sometimes not cut at right angles.

"Machine out of alignment" - Which meant that the folding machine was sometimes out of alignment.

My Ideas and Items to practice at the next team meeting

....

....

PLAN :
DESCRIBE VARIOUS
CAUSES AND IDENTIFY
ROOT CAUSE

Betty said, "Fine. We agree on the three most likely causes. Now we need to know how often these occur. We still need to focus in on the root cause of the angle deviations. We do not have it yet."

The team needed more data. They decided to look at the fourteen cubic containers that were outside of the 1.5 degree angle deviation on the previous Histogram. Those failed inspection and the question was "why". The team decided to determine how often the above three likely causes happened with the failed fasteners. Karen and Ned were familiar with the units because they had just collected the data for the Histogram, so they volunteered to examine the fourteen fasteners. This inspection required only one hour of their time and allowed them to create the following Pareto Chart:

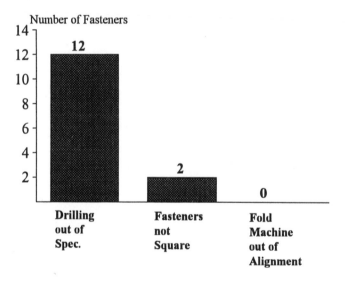

PARETO CHART

Pareto Chart

Page 95 of
Memory Jogger II

Page 143 of
Power-Up

Karen showed the results to Sam who heads the assembly unit. Sam, in turn, asked for help from two operators who construct the fasteners. They had not realized that the fasteners could be causing the problem and gladly agreed to attend the next meeting. That meeting was an historic one for the team. It was held at lunch time in a corner of the cafeteria and the team knew at that meeting that they finally found the root cause.

My Ideas and Items to practice at the next team meeting

....

....

Tree Diagram

At that lunch time meeting, Betty welcomed the operators, Bill and Mark, and thanked them for attending. The meeting had been called so quickly that she did not have time to generate and circulate a P.A.R.T. In an effort to be clear with everyone on the purpose of that meeting, she handed out a sheet of paper that had the proposed purpose on it:

> Purpose: To use the quality tools to uncover the cause of
> drill holes being out of specification limits.

She said at the meeting, "Let's all remember that this is not about looking for a *person* that is at fault. Rather it is about looking for a piece of a *process* that is not right."

Nancy suggested a Tree Diagram and sketched a simple Tree on paper as she asked the question "What are the reasons that can cause drilling to be out of specs?"

Everyone, including the operators said there were really just two reasons. Either the drilling machine needed calibration, or the drill operator was setting the dimensions improperly. Karen placed those on the Tree:

TREE DIAGRAM

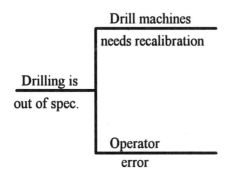

Tree Diagram
Page 156 of Memory Jogger II

Note that a Tree Diagram is commonly used to plan detailed tasks or solutions. In the above case, the team used it differently. They found a Tree Diagram to be useful for identifying and isolating the broad reasons for an error in drilling. As we will see shortly, one of those broad reasons was then used at the head of a Fishbone Diagram. The point here is that they used a Tree Diagram creatively to identify broad areas as a lead-in to a Fishbone Diagram.

My Ideas and Items to practice at the next team meeting

....

....

PLAN :
DESCRIBE VARIOUS
CAUSES AND IDENTIFY
ROOT CAUSE

Nancy asked the operators if they had any data on the frequency of these two possibilities. "How often do each of these occur?" she asked. As the operators talked about their experience in those two areas, Karen made notes on the Tree Diagram:

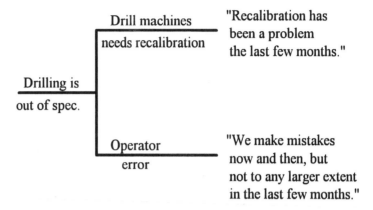

Drilling is
out of spec.

Drill machines
needs recalibration

"Recalibration has
been a problem
the last few months."

Operator
error

"We make mistakes
now and then, but
not to any larger extent
in the last few months."

Karen felt a certain sense of excitement because they were getting closer to the root cause. "Well," she said, "it looks like another Fishbone Diagram can be used here." She drew a Fishbone sketch on paper and explained the basic idea to the two visiting team members. "What are the main categories?" she asked. The team sketched this diagram in less than fifteen minutes:

Cause & Effect
Diagram
Page 23 of
Memory Jogger II
Page 185 of
Power-Up

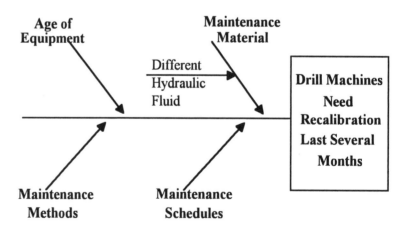

Age of
Equipment

Maintenance
Material

Different
Hydraulic
Fluid

Drill Machines
Need
Recalibration
Last Several
Months

Maintenance
Methods

Maintenance
Schedules

My Ideas and Items to practice at the next team meeting

....

....

The team quickly realized that the only change in the last three months was the hydraulic fluid used in the drill machines. Nothing else had changed. Karen even remembered ordering the standard fluid but receiving the replacement from the supplier. No one had called the supplier simply because there was a note with the different fluid stating that it was an equivalent to the original.

Root Cause
When Karen called the supplier, they faxed a specification sheet on the replacement fluid which showed that under heavy pressure the positioning readings on the drill would not be accurate.

With that information the team wrote the following statement:

> "The hydraulic fluid used in our drilling machines for the
> fasteners is not compatible with our manufacturing process. It
> is the root cause of our high reject rate on cubic container
> because it causes the drilling equipment to be misaligned."

Outcomes and Learning Points of 'Determine Root Cause'
The team entered this step of the investigation simply knowing that fasteners were the main difficulty and that it could be occurring in several different areas of the manufacturing process. They first learned that the difficulty was with the angle of the fasteners. Then they learned the amount of deviation in the angle, which led to focusing on the drilling process. That, in turn, led to the discovery that the fluid in the drilling machines was an incorrect type, and was causing positioning errors.

In this step, the team learned to use data extensively. They relied on data to provide information and clues about the location of the problem. They used the quality tools to display and assist in analysis of the data.

Tools Used

- P.A.R.T.   • Pie Chart   • Pareto Chart

- Histogram   • Matrix Diagram

- Cause-and-Effect Diagram   • Tree Diagram

My Ideas and Items to practice at the next team meeting

PLAN: DEVELOP A SOLUTION

Betty asked the two drill operators, Bill and Mark, to join the team at the next meeting as they developed a solution that would permanently correct this problem, and perhaps prevent others like it from happening. The P.A.R.T. had this purpose statement:

> Purpose: To develop a solution that will prevent the fluid problem with our drill from happening again.

At the lunch time meeting Bill stated that ordering the proper fluid was only half of the solution. They would also have to have a process that ensured that only that fluid was used.

> "We have two other heavy fluids in that shop area," he said, "and I have seen maintenance people refilling oil in machines with the closest oil on hand. We really have to stop that somehow."

Tree Diagram

This time Ned suggested that a Tree Diagram might help them capture the major items for proper maintenance on the drill machines. At first Nancy suggested an Affinity Diagram, but they all agreed that the scope of things that need to be done to prevent a maintenance mishap was narrow, and they could uncover those easily. They constructed the following Tree Diagram in about fifteen minutes:

TREE DIAGRAM
SOLUTIONS TO MAINTENANCE OF DRILLS

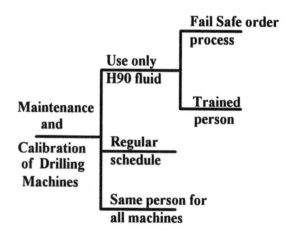

My Ideas and Items to practice at the next team meeting

....

....

They realized that two elements were needed. One was a fail safe order process wherein the proper fluid would be both ordered and received. The other was a way to assure that only that fluid would be actually used in the drilling machines.

Flow Chart
The team constructed the following flow chart for a final safe ordering process:

FLOW CHART
FAIL SAFE ORDERING

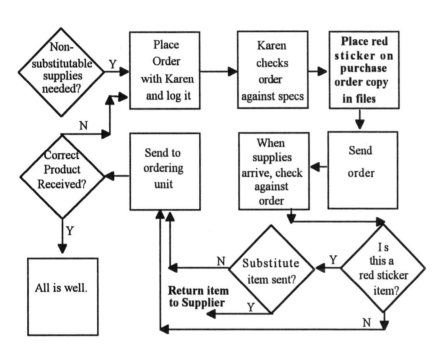

The idea for the red sticker on the file copy of the order came from Mark who said:

> "As long as Karen is in the office when the ordered supplies come in, we're okay. She knows to check it. But if she is out and we have a substitute, that's when we can be in trouble simply because no one tells the substitute what to do. There are far too many things going on in that purchasing department for Karen to think of all of them to tell someone."

My Ideas and Items to practice at the next team meeting

....

....

PLAN :
DEVELOP A
SOLUTION

Karen liked the idea. A red sticker would mean that no substitute could be accepted. This method would apply not only to the H90 fluid, but to any supplies where the original product was a necessity. Every received order would be checked against the order in the file. If a red sticker was present, that product had to meet the order specifications and brand name exactly.

Final Solution and Process Owners
The team had two changes to recommend:

- The Purchasing Process. They saw Karen as the Process Owner, and she agreed.

- Assignment of trained maintenance people in the drilling area. They saw Sam as the Process Owner, and he agreed.

Change in the Purchasing Process
The flow chart on the previous page was supported by the entire team. Karen saw it as a tremendous help to her and an improvement for the ordering of any critical, non-substitutable supplies, not just hydraulic fluid.

Change in Assignment of Maintenance People
Sam agreed to assign only one person and one back-up to the maintenance of the drilling machines. He said that would add some strain on the overall scheduling, but that the need to do it was clear. He also decided that those two maintenance people would have special maintenance training by the equipment manufacturer.

Outcomes and Lessons Learned of 'Develop a Solution'
The team was able to easily use some idea generating and analysis tools to focus on two key solutions. Further, the improvement in the purchasing process would be of benefit throughout the plant, not just for their problem. They also learned the value of bringing in other people, in this case it was Mark and Bill, who are not regular team members but who have expert knowledge and ideas in the area being addressed.

Tools Used

- P.A.R.T.   • Tree Diagram   • Flow Chart

My Ideas and Items to practice at the next team meeting

....

....

DO: IMPLEMENT THE SOLUTION

Karen took charge of implementing the change in the purchasing process. She formed a simple flow chart for herself of the steps she would take to implement this with others in the group:

FLOW CHART
KAREN'S IMPLEMENTATION STEPS

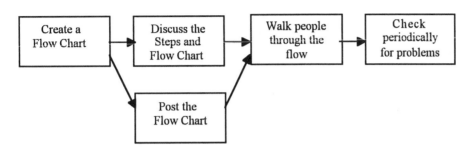

Based on the Flow Chart that the 'Boxing Team' had created, Karen drew a Flow Chart of the steps the purchasing group would use for the "red sticker" items, that is, those that could not have a substitute. She showed that proposed flow to the whole purchasing group and asked them to brainstorm other possibilities. The result was the following:

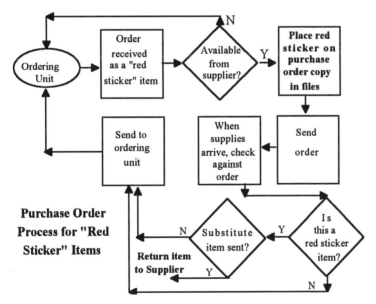

My Ideas and Items to practice at the next team meeting

....

DO :
IMPLEMENT THE
SOLUTION

Karen discussed the new procedure, walked the other people in the purchasing group through it, and even used the procedure with a few trial orders. It was simple and it fit well into their existing methods and filing systems.

Sam easily implemented his part of the solution by selecting two maintenance people, asking them if they would be interested in being fully responsible for maintenance on the drill units, and arranging a training review with the equipment representative.

Both Karen and Sam reported their progress back to the team.

Company Wide Implementation
The team sent a notice to all employees and posted the notice in various places around the plant. That notice informed everyone on the new ordering process. It said:

> "If you are ordering a part, fluid, or any supply item that must be original equipment or a particular brand or type, and substitutes by the supplier are not acceptable, write the words 'red sticker item' at the top of our standard P101 form."

Outcomes and Learning Points of 'Implement a Solution'
The value of writing the sequence of the steps for implementation became clear to Karen, and she shared that with the rest of the team. Her Flow Chart on how to go about the implementation was simple, yet she said that it provided her with a structure that helped her, and helped her fellow workers understand. Further, the purchasing group learned the impact that their process can have on the end product received by the company's customers. The reject rate and the complaints by customers really stemmed from the machine fluid that purchasing ordered. Until this time, that group had no idea of the scope of their actions.

Sam's assembly group was pleased to know that they were receiving help through careful maintenance plans and schedules.

Tools Used

      • Brainstorming   • Flow Chart

My Ideas and Items to practice at the next team meeting

....

....

CHECK: EVALUATE THE SOLUTION
Karen kept a simple Check Sheet of the number of "red sticker" items that were ordered each week. This is what she recorded over the first four weeks after the notice to the whole company:

CHECK : EVALUATE THE SOLUTION

Check Sheet

Page 31 of Memory Jogger II

CHECK SHEET

	Week 1	Week 2	Week 3	Week 4
'Red' Items	III	JHT JHT II	JHT JHT JHT JHT II	JHT JHT JHT IIII
Regular Items	JHT JHT JHT JHT JHT JHT JHT JHT JHT	JHT JHT JHT JHT JHT JHT JHT JHT JHT I	JHT JHT JHT I JHT JHT JHT II JHT JHT JHT III	JHT JHT JHT II JHT JHT JHT JHT JHT JHT III
Total				
Red	3	12	22	19
Regular	45	46	51	50
% Red	7%	26%	43%	38%

Based on this check sheet, she constructed the following chart:

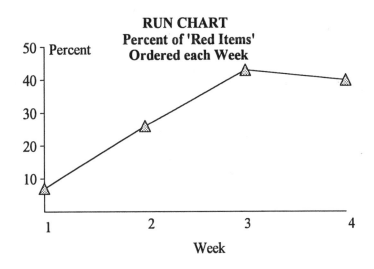

RUN CHART
Percent of 'Red Items'
Ordered each Week

My Ideas and Items to practice at the next team meeting

....

....

CHECK :
EVALUATE THE
SOLUTION

Team Meeting

Betty called a meeting of the team. Included with the notice was a P.A.R.T. that had this purpose statement:

> Purpose: To evaluate the effectiveness of the solution and to decide if any modifications are needed.

She asked the team members to check their work units to see if the new purchase ordering procedure was being used by each unit, and she asked Karen to bring the Run Chart shown on the previous page. Sam was asked to prepare a report for the group on the effectiveness of the maintenance changes.

Karen made these points based on the Run Chart and on conversations with people throughout the plant:

- "There has been a quick awareness of the new process."
- "This new approach has been much needed. Many items must be of a certain type or brand only."
- "Our team solution has benefited the whole plant, not just the assembly unit."
- "I had some concern that work units may be requesting a 'red sticker' treatment unnecessarily. I do not think that is true, but we will continue to track it."

Sam made these points:

- "The special maintenance schedule works well and is not a problem to handle."
- "The maintenance personnel prefer having some specific responsibilities, like this approach provides."
- "I think we as a team have begun a maintenance approach for the drill units that is valuable in other parts of the plant."
- "We have tracked deviations in drill position and in fastener angles and have found great results, as shown on the following Histogram:"

My Ideas and Items to practice at the next team meeting

....

....

CHECK :
EVALUATE THE
SOLUTION

Histogram

Page 66 of
Memory Jogger II

Page 157 of
Power-Up

HISTOGRAM
FASTENER ANGLE, DEGREES FROM VERTICAL

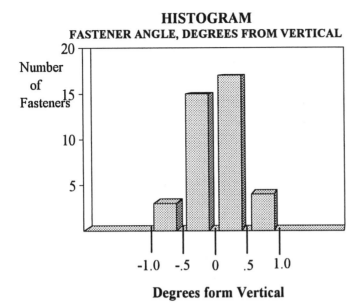

Degrees form Vertical

In addition to seeing the decrease in the angle deviations, the reject rates from inspectors and from customers decreased significantly, and the cost of rework due to the fastener angle problems was virtually eliminated:

PARETO CHART

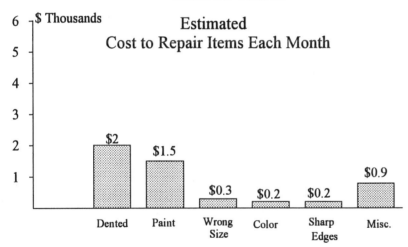

Estimated
Cost to Repair Items Each Month

Type of Complaint

My Ideas and Items to practice at the next team meeting

CHECK :
EVALUATE THE
SOLUTION

With this Histogram, the Run Chart by Karen, and the decreases in reject rates and rework costs reflected by the Pareto Chart, the team clearly saw the success of their efforts.   Furthermore, the team estimated the decrease in rework costs due to these changes will save the company about $55,000 each year.

Outcomes and Learning Points of 'Evaluate the Solution'
The team had measured the success of the changes in both the purchasing process and in the maintenance procedures. Customer complaints were lower, and rework costs were almost cut in half.

Tools Used

• P.A.R.T.   • Histogram   • Run Chart   • Pareto Chart

My Ideas and Items to practice at the next team meeting

....

....

ACT: REFLECT AND ACT ON LEARNINGS

The solution worked well. It showed the following characteristics. It was:

- **D**oable
- **R**ealistic
- **U**nderstandable
- **M**easurable

The team did not modify the solution, but they encouraged the workers in the purchasing group as well as the maintenance personnel in the drill area to make suggestions for further improvement as time went on.

STANDARDIZE

After implementing and evaluating the solutions, the team began to discuss an area that was new for the company. Betty and others had been talking about possible ISO 9000 certification for the company. To be certified they knew that their processes would have to be standardized and documented. Flow Charts and analysis of their work flows were scarce at Global Container Productions, but the standardization of the purchase process and of maintenance procedures was a start. They obtained a copy of the ISO 9000 guidelines and began exploring further steps for standardization of their processes.

CELEBRATION

Karl, the owner of the company was delighted with the work of the team and of all those in the company that assisted through data collection and participation in the solutions. To express his appreciation, he arranged an extended lunch break where he gave a personal thank you to every individual that participated in the effort in any way. He also gave a bonus to each of the team members, pointing out that their efforts saved the company a considerable amount of rework cost and possible lost revenues through customers leaving if the fastener problem had continued.

He also pointed out that they had begun a new journey of managing their work. They had among some of the workers begun using data, charts, and graphs of various kinds to make decisions and to guide their work. Also, they had taken the opportunity to expand that effort into a start at standardization of processes and ISO 9000 certification. They were becoming a new kind of company.

End of Manufacturing Example

My Ideas and Items to practice at the next team meeting

....

About the Author

William L. Montgomery is president of the Montgomery Group, a team of consultants that teach and implement a wide range of techniques, tools, management skills, and planning approaches for improving organizations. He is also an associate of GOAL/QPC in Methuen, Massachusetts, which specializes in research and education for the effective application of TQM in both service and manufacturing organizations. Bill specializes in Effective Strategic Planning, Process Improvement, Team Training, Coaching, and Facilitator Training.

Bill received his Masters and his Doctorate in engineering and biomedical engineering from the University of Pittsburgh after his Bachelors degree from Lehigh University. He also attained a Masters Degree in Management Sciences from Pace University in New York City. He joined Bell Labs in 1968, earning various patents before joining AT&T where he managed systems projects. In 1984 he was asked to organize and design the quality efforts for a business unit of AT&T. Significant improvements were realized through the efforts of twenty facilitators and dozens of process improvement initiatives. He later joined AT&T Corporate Headquarters as an internal consultant and trainer. Before retiring from AT&T, Bill influenced the quality efforts and trained the facilitators of most of the business units in the company. He and his wife Loretta enjoy visiting their four daughters and their families, who live in Florida, North Carolina, Virginia, and Massachusetts.

For more information, please contact

Bill Montgomery
P.O. Box 41
Pittstown, NJ 08867

Business Telephone: 908-479-6673
Fax Transmission: 908-479-6674